# DATE DUE

| | | | |
|---|---|---|---|
| | | | |
| | | | |
| | | | |
| | | | |
| | | | |
| | | | |
| | | | |
| | | | |
| | | | |
| | | | |
| | | | |
| | | | |
| | | | |
| | | | |
| | | | |
| | | | |
| | | | |
| | | | |

Demco, Inc. 38-293

Shop Identity Series Vol.4

# PACKAGE &
# SHOPPING BAG

ショップ アイデンティティ シリーズ Vol.4
パッケージ & ショッピングバッグのデザイン

Shop Identity Series Vol.4
# PACKAGE & SHOPPING BAG

Published in 2008
by BNN, Inc.
35 Sankyo Building 1F
3-7-2 Irifune Chuo-ku Tokyo 104-0042 Japan
fax: +81-3-5543-3108   e-mail: info@bnn.co.jp
www.bnn.co.jp

Designer: Hajime Kabutoya (Happy and Happy)
          Maki Jinzenji (Happy and Happy)
Photographer: Natsu Tanimoto (studio track72)
Translator: Yuko Kamada (R.I.C. Publications)
Editor: Hitoshi Mitomi / Shiyo Yamashita
Editorial Assistant: Kaori Irie

Publisher: Kouichi Yabuuchi

Printing: Kosaido Co., Ltd.

ISBN978-4-86100-554-1
Printed in Japan

# CONTENTS

INTRODUCTION

## はじめに

ショップのセールスプロモーションツールをアイテムごとに紹介する「ショップ アイデンティティ シリーズ」。
第4弾となる本書は、パッケージとショッピングバッグのデザインの、最新事例集です。

箱・包装紙・袋・シール・リボン、またクリスマスなどのシーズン毎・キャンペーン毎の
ショッパーやギフトBOX、箱に添えられるメッセージカードなどなど、「包む」「贈る」をテーマに、
お店の個性が際立つ事例を多数掲載しました。

コンテンツは業種ごとファッション・リビング・フードの3つに大別し、東京のショップを中心にご紹介しています。
コストや環境問題などの制約がある中で、高いデザイン性を持ちつつ、いかに効果的にお店の存在をアピールするか。
ショップおよび商品の販売戦略にパッケージのデザイン力は不可欠であるはずです。

デザイン資料集・アイデアソースとして、デザイナー、ショップ関係者の方々、
またこれからショップを始めようとしている方々まで広く活用いただけましたら幸いです。

本書制作にあたり、多忙中ご協力いただいたショップ関係者の皆様、
快く作品をご提供いただいたクリエイターの皆様に、深くお礼を申し上げます。

# Introduction

The "Shop Identity Series" introduces sales promotion tools for shops and stores.
This fourth collection presents the latest designs of packaging and shopping bags.

The key themes covered are "Wrapping" and "Gift Giving" with
the collection offering a range of products to enhance each shop's individuality.
It includes boxes, wrapping paper, bags, stickers, ribbons as well as shopping bags,
gift boxes and message cards for seasons such as Christmas or any other special campaigns.

This book is divided into three categories; fashion, living and food, and most of the shops
that appear in the book are located in Tokyo. How can you maintain quality design and
effectively advertise your shop when restricted by costs and the need to consider environmental issues?
We believe that packaging design is an essential sales strategy for both shops and products.

We hope designers and those who are involved in shop management, as well as future shop owners,
will find this book a useful resource for designs and ideas.

We wish to express special thanks to all the people who took time from their busy schedule
to help us publish this book and the creators who agreed to let us use their works.

# INTRODUCTION

## ［本書の見方］

●コンテンツアイコン

●ショップ名 　 　●業種

NOJESS ノジェス / アクセサリーと服飾雑貨の販売 Accessory and Fashion Goods Seller
SB: 株式会社サザビーリーグ SAZABY LEAGUE, Ltd. AD（Bag, Tag, Seal）: 岩波眞里 Mari Iwanami
AD（Box）: サザビーリーグ アガット事業部 SAZABY LEAGUE agete Division

●制作クレジット

SB: Submittor 作品提供者

CD: Creative Director クリエイティブディレクター

AD: Art Director アートディレクター

D:Designer デザイナー

P: Photographer フォトグラファー

I: Illustrator イラストレーター

CW: Copywriter コピーライター

ST: Stylist スタイリスト

HM: Hair Make ヘアメイク

DF: Design Firm 制作会社

※上記以外の制作クレジットは略さず記載しています。

※作品提供者の意向により、制作者名を記載していない場合があります。

※「株式会社」「有限会社」は省略させていただきました。

# INTERVIEW
# *&* WORKS

## GROOVISIONS

# GROOVISIONS

## 使う人にとって少しでもその時間が楽しいものになるようなパッケージを

設立から14年を迎えたデザイングループ、グルーヴィジョンズ。

その活躍の場はパッケージや広告、エディトリアルといったグラフィックデザインのクライアントワークから、

オリジナル商品の企画・販売、映像作品の制作と、実に幅広い。

数々の現代美術展に参加するなど作家的な面も併せ持つ彼らだが、デザインに関しての態度は実にストイック。

代表の伊藤 弘氏に話を訊くことができた。

### 大事なのはコンテンツとのバランス

—— 唐突にお聞きしますが、伊藤さんにとって、良くないパッケージとはどういうものですか？

伊藤 弘（以下 I）：一般的にいえばバランスが悪いパッケージでしょうね。何をパッケージするのか、内容物とのバランスが悪いもの。容積的にバランスが悪いのはもちろんだけれども、コストやイメージのバランスもあります。パッケージというのは常にコンテンツがあるものなので、そのコンテンツとの関係性がおかしいものは、面白いかもしれないけれど、あり方として好ましいとはいえない。それを狙っている場合は別ですが。特にクライアントワークの場合は、そういうバランスの悪い面白さを追求したものはやりにくいですね。

—— クライアントワークと、グルーヴィジョンズとしてのオリジナルの仕事、それぞれに取り組む上で意識の面で違いはありますか？

I：特にありません。自分たちで作るものに関しては結局クライアントが自分たちになるというだけで、どのみちデザインのプロセスにおいてはいろいろな制約や条件があるんですよ。その枠組を自分たちで作るか、他の人が作るかという違いだけと思うようにしています。枠組を作る作業というのは、頭の中のどこか別の部分を使って考えているような感じで、それが自分たちにとってすごく良いトレーニングになるんです。そうした作業を繰り返していると、他から与えられた枠組がどういうものなのかがとてもよくわかるようになります。

—— 現在、グルーヴィジョンズにデザイナーは9人いらっしゃると伺いましたが、その中でグルーヴィジョンズとしての共通認識みたいなものは常に共有していらっしゃるのですか？

I：今は僕らに限らず、デザイナーがひとつのスタイルで押し通すのは難しい時代になっていると思っています。現在の僕らの作業は、1つ1つの仕事は常に試行錯誤ですし、特にグルーヴィジョンズとしてのスタイルみたいなものを意識することは少なくなっているようです。それよりも、世間と僕らのやっていることがずれていないかどうか、常にちゃんとはかっていないといけないと思っています。

### 作家的な立場とメインのデザインワークは別物

—— グルーヴィジョンズというとチャッピーの生みの親ということもあって、一般の人々には作家的な部分で判断されることも多いのではないでしょうか。

I：確かに僕らの場合、チャッピーの存在は明らかに大きいので、世間からは作家的な立場を求められることも少なくないのですが、チャッピーやそれにまつわるいろいろなものと、僕らがメインでやってるデザインのクライアントワークというのは、きちんと切り離せていると思います。通常の仕事に対してチャッピー的な要素を求めてくるクライアントである場合でも、僕らの中ではその2つは、いい意味で分離して考えることができるようになりました。

—— では具体的にパッケージについてお聞きしたいのですが、オリジナルのグッズのパッケージに関してはどういうコンセプトがあったのですか？

I：Tシャツ用の箱は、ちょうどTシャツが1枚入るサイズになっているんです。スウェットシャツ用も同じ。これは僕らが店をやる上で、商品そのものがストックになるようなものを考えた結果出てきたデザインです。ただ、最初のバランスの話でいくと、これは若干悪いほうに傾いている。本当はTシャツに対してこんなパッケージは過剰だと思いますし、ストックにももっと合理的な方法があるわけで、でもちょっとバランスが悪いことが面白いからやっているわけです。これは自分たちで枠組を決められる仕事だからこそ出来ることですよね。

—— こちらのガムテープは梱包用に普段から使っているものですか？

I：ガムテープはかなり初期の段階からたくさん作ってきたのですが、これはそのうちのひとつです。梱包するものが何であれ、このテープさえ貼れば自分たちの荷物だっていうのがわかるので便利なんですよね。僕らは自分たちの封筒などは持ってないのですが、これがあればもらった封筒などもリユースできます。

### デザインはコミュニケーションの在り方の設計

—— パッケージ、とくに紙袋みたいなものはすぐに捨てられてしまう類のものですよね。そういうものをデザインする上で、「こうあるべきである」と常に気をつけていることはありますか？

I：捨てられるまでのタームが短いからこそ、使う人にとって少しでもその時間が楽しく、いいものであるように……ということは考えています。あとは使う紙や構造などを含めて、なるべく無駄がないようにすること。そういった配慮が社会的にもかなり重要な条件になってきています。本来なら、もしかしたらなくてもいいかもしれないものを敢えて作っている（P.018へ続く）

OIO

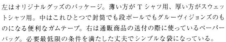

左はオリジナルグッズのパッケージ。薄い方がTシャツ用、厚い方がスウェットシャツ用。中はこれひとつで封筒でも段ボールでもグルーヴィジョンズのものになる便利なガムテープ。右は通販商品の送付の際に使っているペーパーバッグ。必要最低限の条件を満たした丈夫でシンプルな袋になっている。

The item on the left is a package for GROOVISIONS' original goods. The thin container is for a T-shirt and the thick one is for a sweatshirt. Packing tape in the middle is a useful tool for turning envelopes and card boxes into GROOVISIONS' original items. The paper bags on the right are used for mail-orders. It is a tough and simple bag but still meets the minimum necessary requirements.

# Packaging that gives customers fun and enjoyment.

Since the establishment of their business 14 years ago, the design group GROOVISIONS has been involved in an extensive range of work, from graphic design work for packaging, advertising and editorials for clients to the development and sales of their own products. While they have participated in a number of contemporary art exhibitions as creators, they also take their design work for their clients very seriously. Hiroshi Ito, the director of GROOVISIONS gives us some insight on their work.

## The balance between the package and its contents is the key

—This might be an abrupt question, but what sort of packaging do you consider "not very good"?

Hiroshi Ito (HI): Generally speaking, I would say it is difficult to find the right balance with a package and it's contents. This is due to not only the capacity of the package, but the balance between the product, its costs and image also. Naturally, a package is for the contents, so if it is not relevant to what is inside it, even though it might be unusual and intriguing, the package would not be considered very desirable. That is not always the case if it was intended to be different, but a package that focuses on unbalanced uniqueness would not be easy to do successfully, especially for client work.

— Do you take a different approach with your client work compared to your original work?

HI: Not particularly. When it comes to making original products, it just means that we are our own clients and we still have restrictions and conditions in the course of the design process. We think the only difference is whether we set the framework or someone else. Setting a framework is like using a different part of our brain from designing, and it is very good training for us. By repeating this process, it becomes easier for us to understand a framework suggested by someone else.

— I heard that GROOVISIONS has nine designers working at the moment. Do you all share the same perception?

HI: I think that it is not easy for not only us but any designer to persist in just one style these days. As for what we do at the moment, each work is always based on trial and error, and it seems that we are becoming less conscious about a particular style as GROOVISIONS. Rather, I think we should always check if what we are doing is on the right track for the real world.

## Our position as creators is one thing and our main design work another

— Considering GROOVISIONS invented Chappie, does the general public often see you as creators?

HI: It is certainly true that Chappie's effect on us has been so great that we are often expected to take

a role as creators. But we feel confident that we are capable of separating Chappie and things that involves Chappie from our main design work for our clients. Even when clients ask us to include Chappie elements for them, we have now learnt to think separately about these two works in a positive way.

— Now, I want to ask you about your actual packages. What was the concept behind your original goods packages?

HI: A box for a T-shirt is designed to fit just one T-shirt and the same for a sweatshirt. First we thought that if we had our own shop, we would consider each item as stock and keep it that way in our shop. And as a result we came up with this design. But when it comes to a good or bad balance as I told you earlier, it leans to the bad a little bit. I think this kind of package is actually too much for just a T-shirt, and there would be a more practical way to keep stock as well. But we still do it because we think that a little bit of out of balance is interesting, and also we can do it because it is our own project where we can set a framework.

— For this tape, do you usually use it for packing?

HI: We have been making a lot of packing tapes from the beginning and this is one of them. It is useful because whatever the package, we can tell it belongs to us because of the tape. We do not have company envelopes, but we can use envelopes someone gave us just by using this tape. (Continued to Page 018)

CINAGRO ORGANIC KITCHEN & MARKET
Art Direction, Design：グルーヴィジョンズ GROOVISIONS
Interior Design：片山正通（Wonderwall）Masamichi Katayama（Wonderwall）
Client：薬糧開発株式会社 Yakuryokaihatsu.co.,ltd

# CINAGRO

表参道のオーガニック系セレクトショップ
らしく、高級感とナチュラルさが両立
To represent an exclusive organic shop in
Omotesando, this design has both a sense of
high quality and natural taste.

—— ショップツール、ウェブサイトを通じて、テーマカラーは緑と茶で統一されていますが、このカラーリングについて教えてください。

グルーヴィジョンズ（以下 G）：オーガニック食材を扱う店舗ですので、やはりアースカラーをベースに考えました。まず緑色に関しては、ベタ面で使用する際に目を引くよう、明度・彩度ともに高めな色を選択しました。この緑色は店舗内の椅子の座面に張られているファブリックの色にも使用しています。茶色に関しては、緑とは逆にシックでナチュラルなイメージを出すために選びました。

—— 表参道に新規オープンする「GYRE」という商業施設、しかもかなりデザインオリエンテッドなビルの中にできる店舗ということで、特に意識されたことはありますか。

G：このテナントビルの性格上、少なからず高級感やファッション性は必要であると考えました。しかし、そればかりを追求すると、お客様にとって近寄り難い雰囲気を出すイメージになってしまうため、そのバランスをいかに取るかを常に考えながら作業を進めました。

—— 野菜や果物のクラシカルな雰囲気の絵柄と組み合わせられた「C」のロゴマークについて、どのような点に気をつけたか、また狙ったイメージはどういったものだったのかなどを教えて下さい。

G：シンボルマークおよびロゴタイプに関しては、最終案に至る前に数案提案させていただきました。その中ではモダンな案もあり、クリエイティブミーティングの中ではその方向で良いのではという話もあったのですが、テナントビルのイメージからするとややカジュアルに見えてしまう恐れがありました。そのため、「高級感」をクラシカルな絵柄に求め、オーセンティックなイメージが出るようにしました。

—From their shop tools to their website, green and brown are used as theme colors. How did you come up with this combination?

GROOVISIONS (G): As the shop sells organic groceries, it was natural to think about earthy colors as a base. For the green, we chose a hue that is high in brightness and saturation so that it would attract attention when used on a solid surface. The same green fabric is used to upholster chairs in the shop as well. We chose the brown to create a chic and natural image, which contrasts with the green.

— The shop is in "GYRE", a new commercial facility in Omotesando. Considering the fact that it is a quite design-oriented building, is there anything you were particularly conscious of?

G: Because of the characteristics of the building, we thought it needed to have some high-class quality and be fashionable. But if we focused on those elements too much, it would create an unapproachable image to customers. So we were always thinking about how to keep a good balance when working on the products.

G: The shop logo "C" is combined with pictures of vegetables and fruits in classic way.

— Could you tell me what sort of things you were conscious of and what sort of image you wanted to create?

G: We suggested several different types of symbols and logotypes before making the final decision. Some of them were modern, and at our creative meeting, we thought modern taste might be the right one. But then, there were some concerns that it might look too casual for the image of the building. Considering those aspects, we looked for a classic design with "high-class quality" that creates an authentic image.

販売商品に関してはVI計画で決定したテーマカラー及びタイプフェイスを使用、あまり華美にならないようなデザインを提案。紙袋には瓶詰めなど重量がある商品の展開があるため、やや厚めのクラフト紙を使用している。

The theme colors and typeface chosen for the VI project were used for merchandise, and they suggested that the design should not be too luxurious. Thicker craft paper durable enough for heavy products such as bottled items was used.

100%ChocolateCafe.
Art Direction, Design：グルーヴィジョンズ GROOVISIONS
Interior Design：片山正通（Wonderwall）Masamichi Katayama（Wonderwall）
Produce：アンドーギャラリー ANDO GALLERY,INC.
Client：明治製菓株式会社 MEIJI SEIKA KAISHA., LTD

014

# 100%ChocolateCafe.

内装のクールさに親しみやすさを加味
綿密な色彩計画で愛されるパッケージに

Adds friendliness to the coolness of the interior
A careful color scheme makes a package that
every body loves.

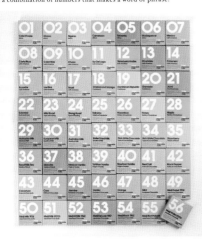

種類ごとにナンバリングされたパッケージ。当初はコレクション欲をくすぐることも考慮に入れていたそうだが、今では色の組み合わせだけで商品を選ぶのではなく、記念日や語呂合わせからなる数字の組み合わせで購入するユーザーも増えているという。

Packages are numbered to match the chocolates. At first they hoped it might encourage customers to collect all the numbers, but they found out that they now buy the products that match their anniversary date or by a combination of numbers that makes a word or phrase.

――この店に関しては様々なクリエイターの方が集まって一つの世界を作り上げていくという形が取られていたようですが、特にデザインプロデューサーの安東孝一さんから方向性についての指示はありましたか。

G：我々を推薦して下さったのは安東さんと（インテリアデザイン担当の）片山正通さんなのですが、安東さんからは片山さんのクールでシャープな「かっこいい」インテリアデザインの中に、「愉しさ」「温もり」「親しみやすさ」を入れて欲しいとリクエストされました。

――テーマカラーの水色と茶色について。

G：チョコレートがテーマの店舗なので「茶色」は外せないと考えました。そこで茶色と相性の良い色を何色か候補に挙げ、その中でクールでありつつ、丸みを帯びたロゴタイプとの組み合わせで一番しっくりきた水色を加えた2色をショップカラーとして提案しました。食品を扱う店舗やパッケージに寒色を使用することは業界内でタブーということを以前聞いたことがあり、やや不安だったのですが、逆にそのことで他店との差別化を図ることができ、またそのカラーリングによってショッピングバッグにもファッション性が加味され、街中でも埋もれること無く目を引く結果となりました。

—I understand that this project took a number of creators. Were there any suggestions from Koichi Ando, the design producer, about which direction you were heading to?

G: It was Mr. Ando and Mr. Masamichi Katayama (in charge of interior design) who recommended us, and Mr. Ando asked us to add "fun", "warmth" and "friendliness" to Mr. Katayama's "stylish" interior design with its cool and sharp taste.

— About the theme colors of blue and brown.

G: It is a chocolate shop, so we thought " brown" was a must color and then picked some other colors that go well with brown. Among those colors, the blue looked best when combined with the cool yet rounded-shape logotype, so we suggested the blue and brown as theme colors. We were a little concerned about using the blue because we heard that it is taboo to use a cold color for shops and packaging that involves food. But, on the contrary, it turned out to be a success in differentiating it from other shops. The color combination also made the shopping bags look more fashionable, drawing attention outside.

「100%ChocolateCafe.」のプロジェクトがスタートしたのは 2003 年。グルーヴィジョンズは翌年初夏頃から参加したが、当初の依頼は VI 計画の核となるロゴタイプの制作だったという。4 案ほど提案した中ではほぼ現状に近い案が採用され、その後は開店までの約半年間でショッピングバッグや紙コップ、マグカップなど店舗で使用されるアイテムのデザインが進められた。

The "100%ChocolateCafe" project started in 2003, and GROOVISIONS joined in early summer of the following year. At first they were asked to create a logotype, which was the core element of VI project. The current logo was chosen among the four suggestions they made, and the design has not been changed much since the selection. For the following six months, they worked on designing shop items including shopping bags, paper cups and mug cups.

—— 56 種類のチョコレートに対して 8 色のパッケージが用意されています。

G：当初は「全て異なる色で」というご要望でしたが、そうなると色の組み合わせが困難になり、またディスプレイした際に全体的に色味が散漫になり印象がぼやける恐れがあったため、色数を 56 の約数の「8」に制限。次に内装に合い、ディスプレイした際に並びが美しく見え、さらにお客様に「味」だけではなく「色」の組み合わせで選んでいただくことを想定し、どの組み合わせでも違和感ないよう選択したのが現状の 8 色です。

—— チョコレートにナンバリングされている理由は？

G：店舗内の壁面冷蔵ショーケースにディスプレイされている 56 種類のチョコレート生地が明治製菓の製造技術の高さを示し、また片山さんが掲げたインテリアデザインのコンセプトである「シェフズキッチン」を物語っています。「56 種類のチョコレート」はそういった背景を元に生まれた商品であるため、フェースデザインに関しては「味」をメインに開発していくのではなく「キッチンで使用しているチョコレートをお客様に特別にお分けする」といったストーリーを仮想し、業務用の製造番号らしく数字が立つようなデザインでの展開を考えました。

— There are 8 different color packages for 56 kinds of chocolates.

G: At the beginning, the client requested "different colors for each chocolate", but we thought that would make it difficult to match colors. Also, too many colors on display would leave a vague impression of the shop as a whole, so we limited it to 8 colors, which is a divisor of 56. In choosing the eight colors, we set as criteria that they would match the interior design and look beautiful on display. We also wanted customers to choose the products by not only the "taste" of the chocolates but also by the "color" match, so we chose colors that look good however they are combined.

— Why did you put the numbers on the chocolates?

G: The 56 chocolates displayed in the refrigerated showcase on the walls indicate the high quality of Meiji seika's manufacturing technology and represent the "chef's kitchen" that Mr. Katayama suggested as an interior design concept for the shop. With this concept, we thought of a typeface focusing not on the "taste" but on a story telling that "a chef is especially sharing with his customers the chocolates he uses in the kitchen", and we created a design to emphasize the numbers, just like a manufacturer's serial numbers for professional use.

スパイラルによる、「人と人との出会い、コミュニケーション」をテーマにしたプレゼントのオンラインショップ「スパイラルオンラインストア」用に制作したラッピングペーパー。「Thank You」「Merry Christmas」「Happy Birthday」など定番メッセージが一枚に詰め込まれている。http://store.spiral.co.jp
This wrapping paper was made for "Spiral Online Store". The theme of this online gift store is "Encounters and Communication". "Thank you", "Merry Christmas", "Happy Birthday", all these standard messages are expressed on one paper. http://store.spiral.co.jp

スパイラルオンラインストア　オリジナルラッピングペーパー　Spiral Online Store original wrapping paper
Art Direction, Design：グルーヴィジョンズ　GROOVISIONS　Client：スパイラル / 株式会社ワコールアートセンター　Spiral / Wacoal Art Center

（P.010 からの続き）わけだから、少しでも（在り方として）正しいものであったり、人の気持ちが良くなるものでないと、今の時代に作る意味がないので。もちろんショッピングバッグに関しては広告媒体の役割も担っているので、ショップの外、街中での見え方ということも重要になってきますが。

── 今後、グルーヴィジョンズとして目指していくものというと何になりますか？
I：僕らに目標があるとすれば、「デザインをするという行為を続ける」ということでしょうね。それが実はすごく大変なことだと思っています。ただ単に漠然と仕事としてデザインをやっているだけでは続かないような気がするし、続けるためには相当いろいろな試行錯誤が必要となるでしょう。デザイン、とくにグラフィックデザインの行為というのは、最終的には人と人とのコミュニケーションの在り方を設計することであり、デザインのためのデザインではないということを常に心がけていないと、どこか変な方向に行ってしまう気がします。それと、コミュニケーションの取り方は変わらないようでいて、時代によって変わっていくものだということも理解していないといけないでしょう。僕らは自分たちの作家性を貫き通すというスタイルというよりはむしろ、違う形でのアプローチの方法を選択している人間です。常にその時代に合った、よりよいコミュニケーションの方法を開発できればと思っています。

(From Page 010) **Designing is to develop the way we communicate**

—Packages, especially paper bags, are something that gets thrown away very quickly. Do you have anything particular on your mind when designing things like that? For example, "it should be made this way"?
HI: One thing is that because it is such a short-lived item, I want the time of using it to be as pleasant and valuable as possible. Another thing is to avoid waste including paper we use too. These are becoming more important considerations from a social point of view. Frankly speaking, we are producing something that might not be necessary. So it would be meaningless if the way we make them is wrong or if we cannot make people happy. Of course, as shopping bags are used as an advertising tool, how they look outside or in downtown locations is also an important factor we need to consider.

—What is GROOVISIONS' aim in the future?
HI: If we have one, it would be "to keep designing". I think it is actually a very challenging task. I do not think you can go on just by creating designs mindlessly as mere work. It would require a lot of trial and error to continue. Design, especially graphic design, is ultimately to develop the way of communication between people. It is not design for design's sake. If we do not keep that in our mind, we might end up going in a peculiar direction. We also need to understand that, although it seems unchanged, how we communicate with each other does change over time. We are a group of people who choose to use a different approach than simply persisting in own style as creators. I hope that we would develop a better way to communicate to suit the time we live in.

グルーヴィジョンズ
〒153-0065　東京都目黒区中町1-11-10
tel 03-5723-6558　fax 03-7568-6179　http://www.groovisions.com

GROOVISIONS
1-11-10 Naka-Cho, Meguro-Ku, TOKYO #153-0065
tel 81-(0) 3-5723-6558　fax 81-(0) 3-7568-6179
http://www.groovisions.com

# FASHION
## 019 - 058

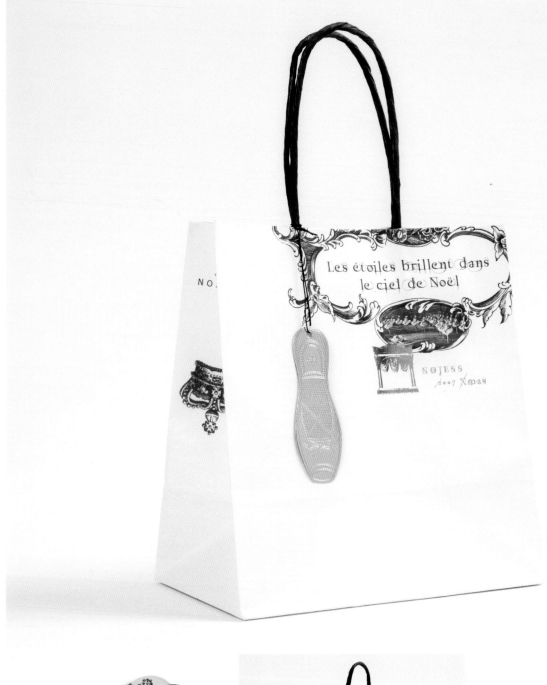

# NOJESS
ノジェス / アクセサリーと服飾雑貨の販売 Accessory and Fashion Goods Seller

SB: 株式会社サザビーリーグ SAZABY LEAGUE, Ltd.　AD（Bag, Tag, Seal）: 岩波眞里 Mari Iwanami
AD（Box）: サザビーリーグ アガット事業部 SAZABY LEAGUE agete Division

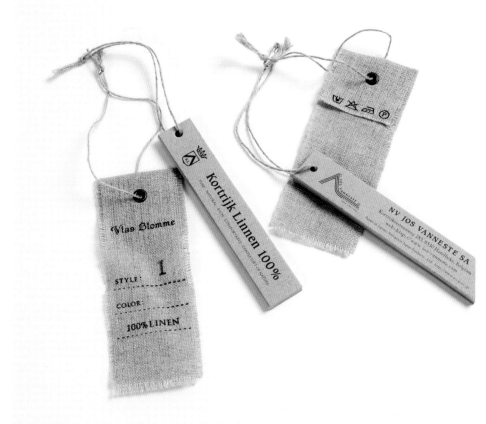

# Vlas Blomme　ヴラス ブラム / アパレルブランド　Apparel Brand

SB: アテンション・ジャパン・プロダクツ有限会社　ATTENTION JAPAN PRODUCTS. LTD　D: A.J.P デザインチーム　A.J.P Design team

# CERASUS ケラスス / アクセサリーブランド Accessory Brand

SB: アテンション・ジャパン・プロダクツ有限会社 ATTENTION JAPAN PRODUCTS. LTD   D: A.J.P デザインチーム  A.J.P  Design team

# LUXEDESIGNS ルクスデザイン / アイウェアの製造・販売 Eyewear Supplier

SB: 株式会社ジェイアイエヌ JIN CO.,LTD　CD, AD, D, P, CW: 呉屋奈奈 Nana Goya
DF: 株式会社ジェイアイエヌクリエイティヴ Div.　JIN CO.,LTD Creative Div.

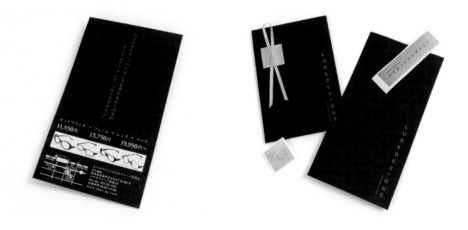

025

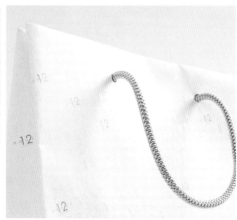

# DOUZE 12 AOYAMA　ドゥーズ 12 青山 / 時計の販売　Watch Brand
SB, DF: オジデザインワークス株式会社　ozi design works inc.

# ESTNATION エストネーション / 大型専門店 Speciality Store

SB: 株式会社エストネーション　ESTNATION INC.　CD: 松原 健（オープラス）Ken Matsubara（OPLUS）

**e.m.** イー・エム / アクセサリー・インテリアグッズの製造・販売 Accessory & Interior Furnishings Supplier

SB, DF: イー・エム・デザイン株式会社 e.m. design Co.,Ltd.　CD: 飛田眞義　Masayoshi Tobita　D: 大森智哉　Tomoya Omori

# Cours de Couleur クールドゥクルール / アクセサリー・小物の販売 Accessory and Fashion Goods Supplier

SB: 株式会社ジェイアイエヌ JIN CO.,LTD  CD, AD, CW: 野澤恭子 Kyoko Nozawa  CD, AD, D, P: 呉屋奈奈 Nana Goya
DF: 株式会社ジェイアイエヌ クリエイティヴ Div.  JIN CO.,LTD Creative Div.

# LOWRYS FARM  ローリーズ ファーム / ブティック  Boutique

SB, DF: 有限会社パンゲア  PANGAEA ltd.   AD, D: 青木康子  Yasuko Aoki

continues >>>

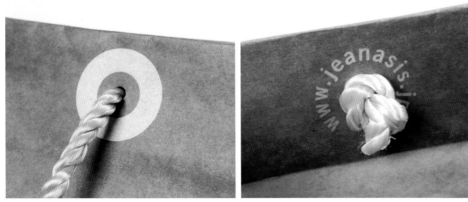

# JEANASIS ジーナシス / ブティック Boutique
SB, DF: 有限会社パンゲア PANGAEA ltd. AD, D: 青木康子 Yasuko Aoki

apart by lowrys　アパート バイ ローリーズ / ブティック　Boutique

SB, DF: 有限会社パンゲア　PANGAEA ltd.　AD, D: 青木康子　Yasuko Aoki

036

continues >>>

038

eu エウ / ブティック Boutique
SB, DF: 株式会社マーク Mark Co., ltd.　CD, AD, D: 伊藤 勇 Isamu Ito

039

n° 11　ナンバー11 / レディスウェアの企画・販売　Ladieswear Supplier
SB: 株式会社シマムラトーキョー・コーポレーション　Shimamura Tokyo Corporation　CD: 嶋村公子　Kimiko Shimamura

040

# H.P.FRANCE Galerie
アッシュ・ペー・フランス ギャラリー
バッグ・小物・アクセサリーの販売　Bag, Fashion Goods and Accessory Supplier
SB: アッシュ・ペー・フランス株式会社　H.P.FRANCE S.A.
D: 野川はるか　Haruka Nogawa

042

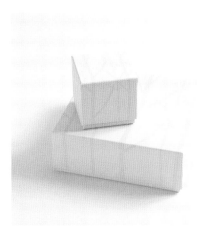

## Kioku H.P.FRANCE

記憶 H.P.FRANCE

バッグ・小物・アクセサリーの販売　Bag, Fashion Goods and Accessory Supplier
SB: アッシュ・ベー・フランス株式会社　H.P.FRANCE S.A.
CD: 村松孝尚　Takanao Muramatsu　D: 佐野智子　Satoko Sano

## Theatre H.P.FRANCE

テアトル アッシュ・ベー・フランス

靴・バッグ・アクセサリー・小物の販売　Shoes, Bag, Fashion Goods and Accessory Supplier
SB: アッシュ・ベー・フランス株式会社　H.P.FRANCE S.A.
CD: 関口 元　Hajime Sekiguchi　D: 佐野智子　Satoko Sano

## HAKKA NIBUN no ICHI

ハッカニブンノイチ / ブティック Boutique
SB, DF: オジデザインワークス株式会社 ozi design works inc

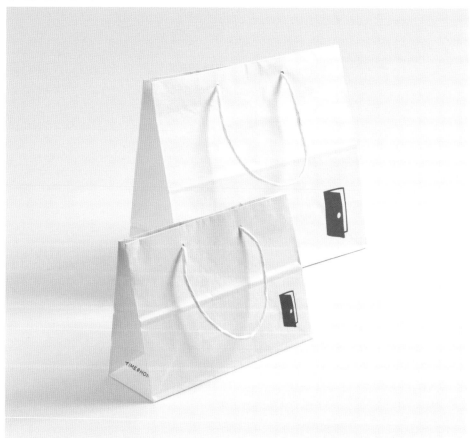

## TIME@HOME

タイム アット ホーム
レディスウェア・生活雑貨の販売 Ladieswear and Homeware Supplier
SB: アッシュ・ベー・フランス株式会社 H.P.FRANCE S.A.
D: 藤本絵里奈 Erina Fujimoto

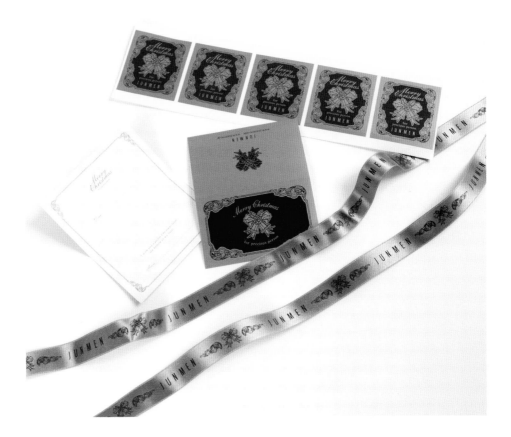

# JUNMEN

ジュンメン / ブティック Boutique
SB: 株式会社ジュン JUN CO.,LTD.
D: 有限会社セメントプロデュースデザイン
CEMENT PRODUCE DESIGN CO.,LTD.

# Adam et Ropé アダム エ ロペ / ブティック Boutique

SB: 株式会社ジュン JUN CO.,LTD. D（A）：ムートンチャック Mouton Chuck D（B）：山縣良和 Yoshikazu Yamagata D（P048 ～ 049）：セミトランスペアレント・デザイン Semitransparent Design
A は 2006 年、B は 2007 年のクリスマス用ショッパー。

046

A

B

A

B

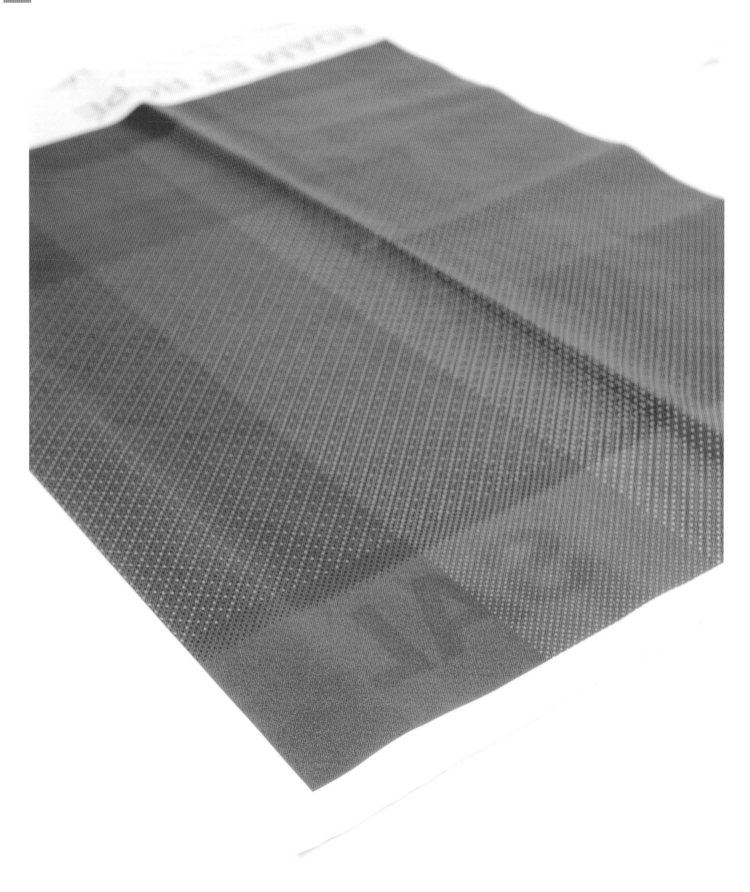

048

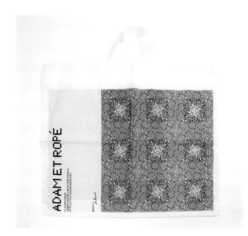

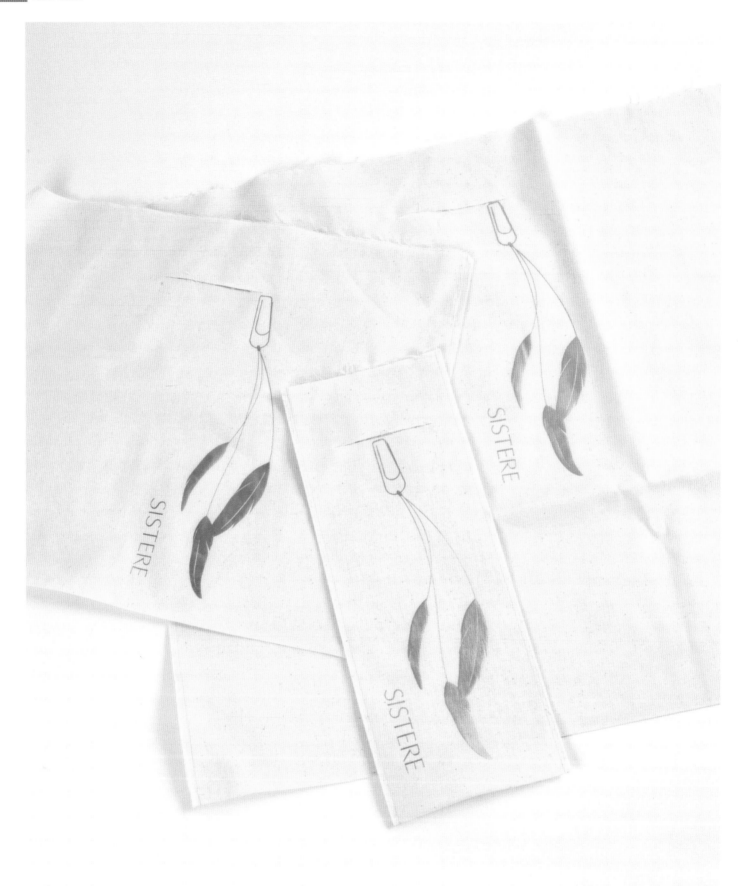

# MANSION OF OWLS マンション・オブ・オウルズ / ブティック Boutique

SB, DF: テン デザイン ラボ ten design lab　AD, D: 宮野琢也 Takuya Miyano

bijou ビジュ / ブティック Boutique

SB, D, DF: デザイン オフィス アンダ  design office anda   CD: 有限会社グラマラス  GLAMOROUS co.,ltd.

en-Fantree アンファントレ / 子供服・小物の販売  Children's Wear Supplier

SB, DF: オジデザインワークス株式会社  ozi design works inc.

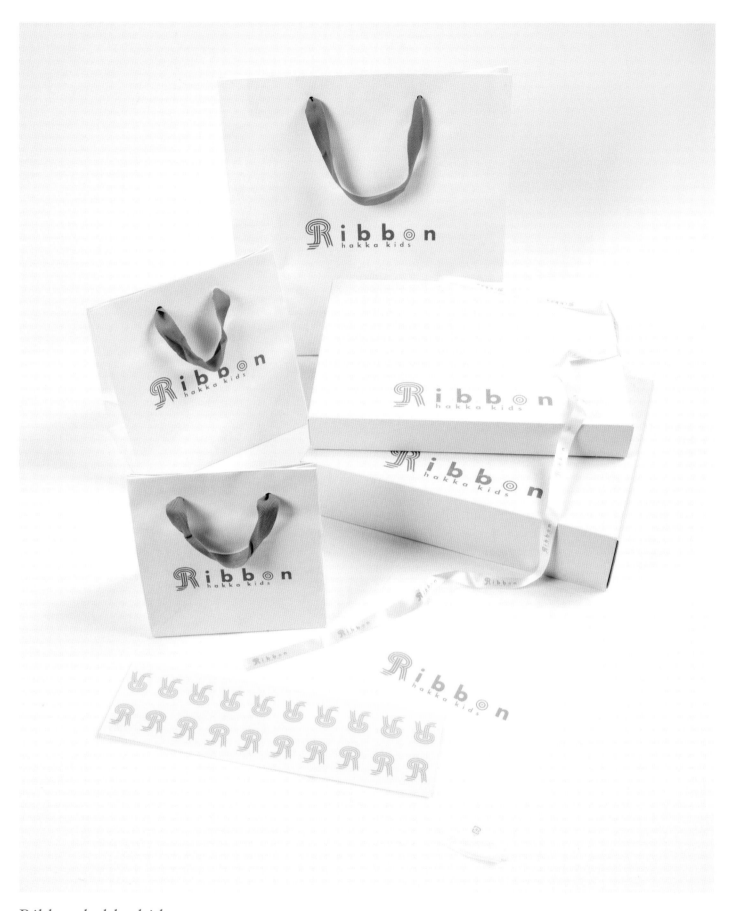

Ribbon hakka kids リボンハッカキッズ / 子供服の販売 Children's Wear Supplier

SB: 株式会社ファッション須賀 Fashion Suga Co.,Ltd.　CD: 葉山啓子 Keiko Hayama　Logo Design: 株式会社シャワーズ Showers Co.,Ltd.

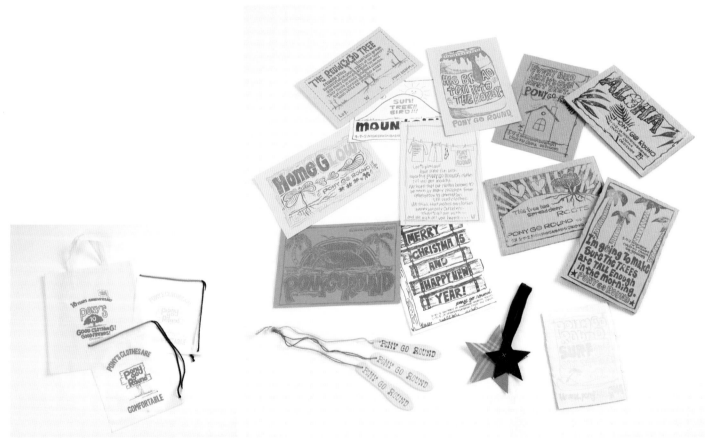

# PONY GO ROUND  ポニー ゴー ラウンド / 子供服の販売  Children's Wear Supplier

SB: ポニー ゴー ラウンド  PONY GO ROUND  D: 長谷部 玲  Rei Hasebe

Zoff ゾフ / メガネ店 Eyewear Supplier

SB: 株式会社インターメスティック Intermestic Inc.　CD (A, B): 園田美紀 Miki Sonoda　CD, AD, D (C): 遠藤 滋 Shigeru Endo
D (A, B): 廣田陽子 Yoko Hirota　P (C): 大竹 泉 Izumu Otake　DF (C): 株式会社ヤード Yard Co.,Ltd.　※ A, B: クリスマス用、キャンペーン用　※ C: 通常ショッパー

# VULCAIN   ヴァルカン / 時計の販売  Watch Sales

SB, DF: 有限会社 美澤修デザイン室  osamu misawa design room Co.,Ltd.    CD, AD: 美澤 修  Osamu Misawa   D, I: 梶谷聡美  Satomi Kajitani

# LIVING
059 - 114

カリモク60 **karimoku 60** / 家具・雑貨店 Furniture & Homeware Store

CL: カリモク家具販売株式会社 KARIMOKU Inc. SB, DF: ドローイングアンドマニュアル有限会社 drawing and manual Inc.
CD, AD: ナガオカケンメイ Kenmei Nagaoka D：中山寛 Hiroshi Nakayama (drawing and manual)

60
VISION

continues >>>

062

包装紙　Wrapping Paper

063

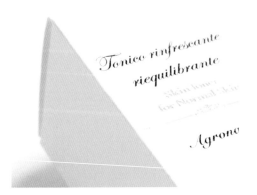

Agronatura アグロナチュラ／本格派自然派化粧品の販売　Natural Cosmetics Supplier

SB: 株式会社イデアインターナショナル　IDEA INTERNATIONAL CO.,LTD.　AD, D: 得能正人　Masato Tokuno

*Latte detergente*
*per tutti i tipi di pelle*
*Olio Lavante*

Cleansing Milk

*Agronatura*

125 ml e
MADE IN ITALY

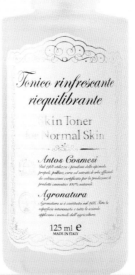

*Tonico rinfrescante*
*riequilibrante*

Skin Toner
for Normal Skin

*Antos Cosmesi*
*Dal 1988 utilizza i prodotti delle apicole:*
*propoli, polline, cera ed estratti di erbe officinali*
*da coltivazioni certificate per la produzione di*
*prodotti cosmetici 100% naturali.*

*Agronatura*
*Agronatura si è costituita nel 1988. Tutte le*
*superficie interessata è tutte le aziende*
*applicano i metodi dell'agricoltura.*

125 ml
MADE IN ITALY

*Tonico rinfrescante*
*riequilibrante*

Skin Toner
for Normal Skin

*Agronatura*

125 ml e
MADE IN ITALY

continues >>>

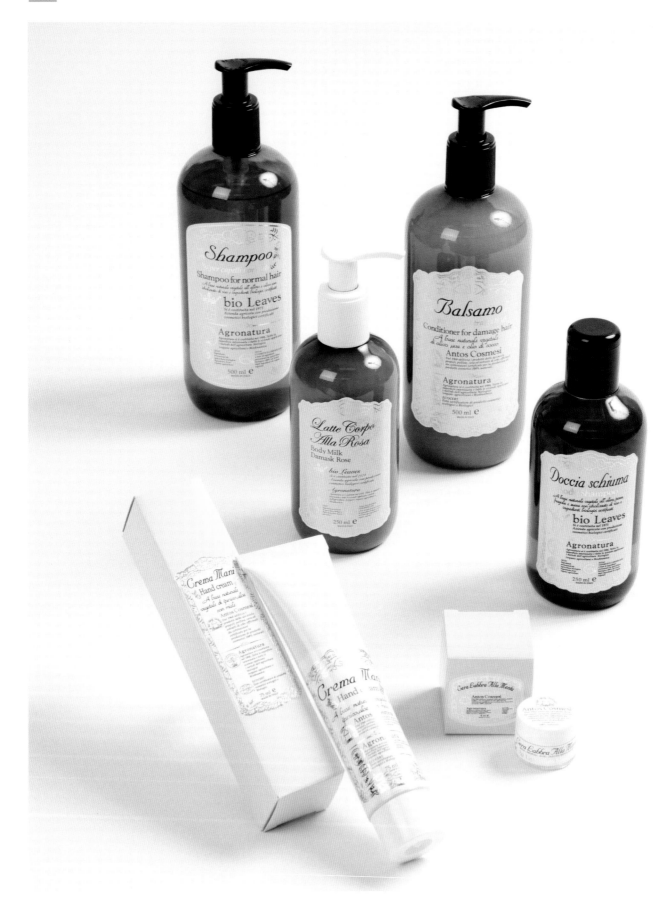

actus kids store　アクタスキッズストア / 子供向け家具・玩具・本などの販売　Children's Furniture, Toys and Books Store

SB, CD, D（Aの巾着袋のみ）: 株式会社アクタス　ACTUS Co.,Ltd.　DF: 株式会社 HD Lab　HD Lab Inc.　CD, C: 宮崎 真（モノタイプ）Makoto Miyazaki（monotype）
AD: 久住欣也　Yoshinari Hisazumi　D: 前川朋徳　Tomonori Maekawa / 中平恵理　Eri Nakadaira / 中岡 舞　Mai Nakaoka　P: 横浪 修　Osamu Yokonami

068

A

Stylist: 轟木節子（FLAT）Setsuko Todoroki（FLAT）  Interior Stylist: 作原文子 Fumiko Sakuhara  Hair Make-Up: 池田慎二（mod's hair）Shinji Ikeda（mod's hair）
Coordinator: 遠藤崇行（jet state）Takayuki Endo（jet state）

A

# ACTUS  アクタス / インテリアショップ  Interior Design Shop

SB, CD, D（Aの大きい紙袋のみ）: 株式会社アクタス  ACTUS Co.,Ltd.  DF: 株式会社 HD Lab  HD Lab Inc.
CD, AD: 久住欣也  Yoshinari Hisazumi  D: 前川朋徳  Tomonori Maekawa / 坂口智彦  Tomohiko Sakaguchi

Délier IDÉE  デリエ イデー / ギフト雑貨店  Gift Shop

SB: 株式会社イデー  IDÉE CO.,LTD.  CD: 神田麻美子  Mamiko Kanda  AD: 森本直樹  Naoki Morimoto

IDÉE shop  イデーショップ / インテリアショップ  Interior Design Shop

SB: 株式会社イデー  IDÉE CO.,LTD.   CD: 神田麻美子  Mamiko Kanda   AD: 森本直樹  Naoki Morimoto

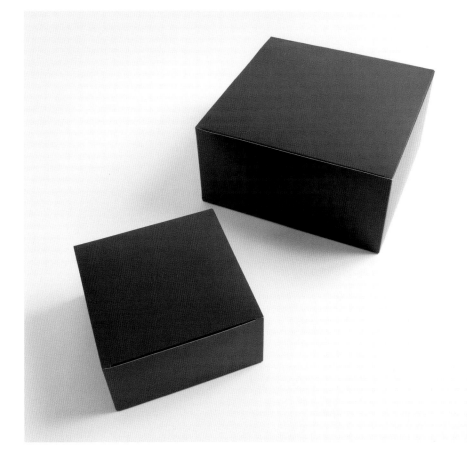

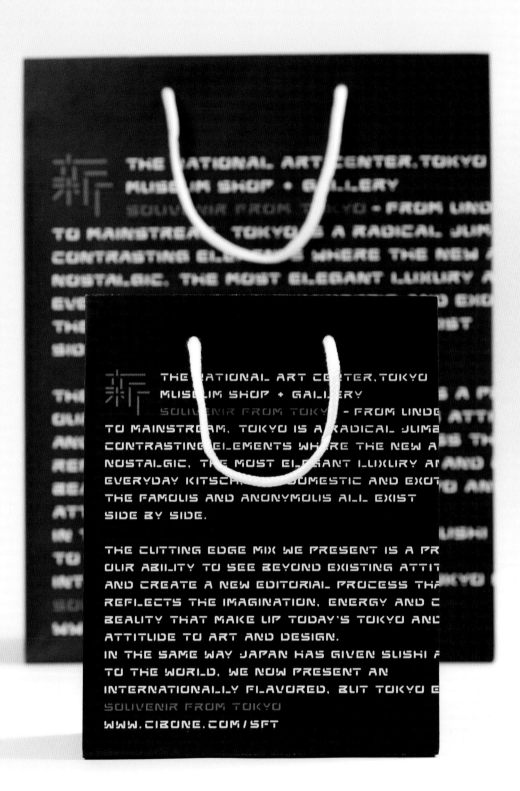

# SOUVENIR FROM TOKYO
スーベニアフロムトーキョー / ミュージアムショップ Museum Gift Shop

SB: スーベニアフロムトーキョー SOUVENIR FROM TOKYO D: 佐藤可士和 Kashiwa Sato

TIME & STYLE　タイム アンド スタイル / インテリアショップ　Interior Design Shop
SB: 株式会社プレステージ ジャパン　PRESTIGE JAPAN INC.　D: タイム アンド スタイル　TIME & STYLE

076

SB: 株式会社中川政七商店　Nakagawa Masashichi Shouten Co., Ltd.

# D&DEPARTMENT PROJECT / 家具・雑貨の販売 Furniture & Homeware Store

SB, DF: ドローイングアンドマニュアル有限会社 drawing and manual Inc.　CD, AD, D: ナガオカケンメイ　Kenmei Nagaoka

CÏBONE  シボネ / インテリアショップ  Interior Design Shop
SB,D: シボネ　CÏBONE　D: 土井宏明（有限会社ポジトロン）Hiroaki Doi（POSITRON INC.）

082

GEORGE'S　ジョージズ / インテリアショップ　Interior Design Shop
SB: 株式会社ジョージズファニチュア　George's Furniture Co., Ltd.

086

## Idea Seventh Sense
イデアセブンスセンス / インテリアショップ  Interior Design Shop
SB: 株式会社イデアインターナショナル  IDEA INTERNATIONAL
AD, D: 得能正人  Masato Tokuno

## Idea Frames
イデアフレイムス / インテリアショップ  Interior Design Shop
SB: 株式会社イデアインターナショナル  IDEA INTERNATIONAL CO., LTD.
AD, D: 福地 掌  Sho Fukuchi
DF: 株式会社サン・アド  SUN-AD COMPANY LIMITED

088

## Idea Digital Code

イデアデジタルコード / インテリアショップ  Interior Design Shop
SB: 株式会社イデアインターナショナル  IDEA INTERNATIONAL
AD, D: 宮崎直理  Naori Miyazaki

## Idea Frames / Idea Seventh Sense / Idea Digital Code

イデアフレイムス / イデアセブンスセンス / イデアデジタルコード
インテリアショップ  Interior Design Shop
SB: 株式会社イデアインターナショナル  IDEA INTERNATIONAL
AD, D: 高橋瑠美  Rumi Takahashi
3業態共通の2007年クリスマス用ショッパー。

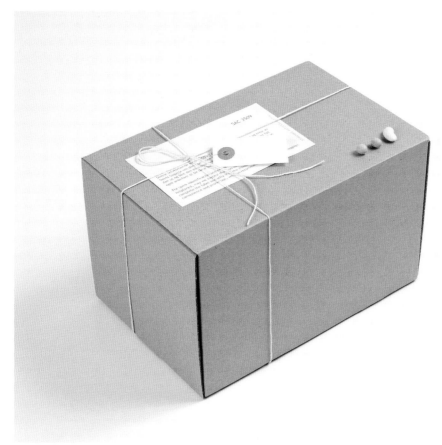

STANDARD ARTICLE : cholon.　スタンダード アーティクル ショロン / 雑貨店 General Goods Store

SB: 有限会社ドゥクール　douxcoeur inc.

cholon 01 STORE　ショロン ゼロワン ストア / 雑貨店　General Goods Store

SB: 有限会社ドゥクール　douxcoeur inc.

trottoir 3　トロトワール / 雑貨店　General Goods Store
SB: 有限会社ドゥクール　douxcoeur inc.

ANGERS　アンジェ / 雑貨店　Life Design Shop

SB: アンジェ　ANGERS　AD: 廣瀬久美子　Kumiko Hirose　D: 中野麻子　Asako Nakano

093

まめぐい　MAMEGUI / 雑貨の販売　General Goods Store

SB: 株式会社かまわぬ　KAMAWANU Inc.

094

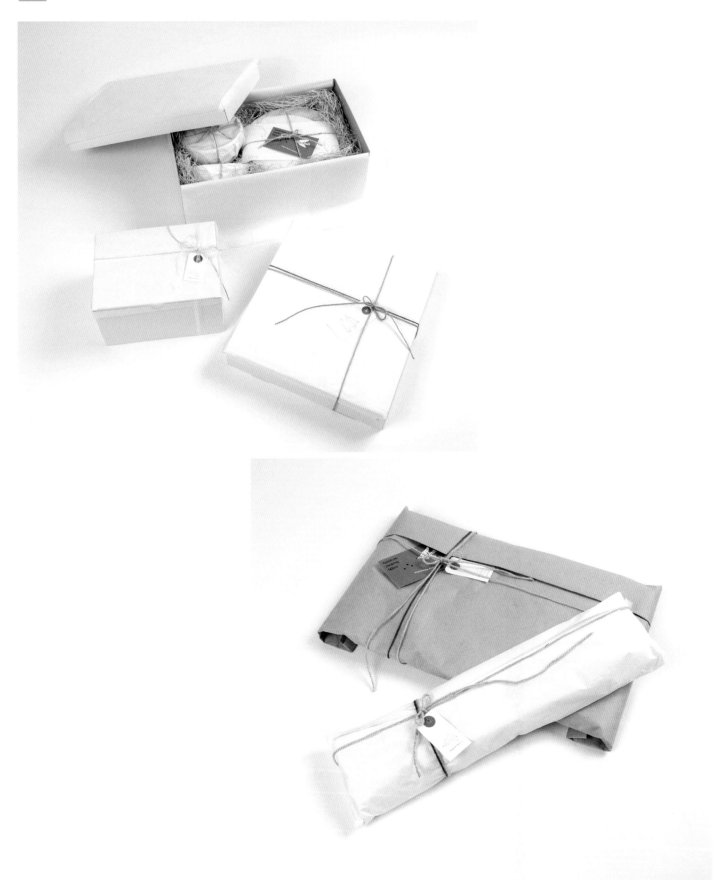

**mishim**  ミシン / オリジナルの家具と雑貨の制作販売  Original Furniture & Homeware Store
SB: ミシン  mishim  CD, AD, D: 土肥牧子  Makiko Dohi
D: 野中かおり  Kaori Nonaka  Graffic Designer: 伊藤ひろこ  Hiroko Ito

096

CINQ / CINQ plus  サンク / サンク・プリュス / 雑貨店  General Goods Store

SB, DF: サンク・デザイン  CINQ DESIGN  AD, D: 保里正人  Masato Hori
左上のショッピングバッグ以外の保存缶は商品パッケージではなく、オリジナル商品として販売しているもの

098

...lat
...
cao

Chocolat
Noir
86%
de cacao

Retirer du feu
puis ajouter
le sucre
vanillé et la
crème fraîche

Casser le chocolat
en morceaux,
ajouter le beurre
et le lait : les
laisser fondre en
remuant avec une
cuillère en bois

A

# Baden Baden バーデンバーデン / デザイン作品の小売　Designer Goods Supplier

SB,AD,D（A-B）：有限会社バーデンバーデン　Baden Baden Inc.　AD,D（C）：セキユリヲ（ea / サルビア）Yurio Seki（ea / Salvia）
CW（C）：木村衣有子　Yuko Kimura

102

B

C

Raconte-moi  ラコンテ・モア / ライフスタイル・ショップ  Lifestyle Shop

SB: 株式会社藤栄  FUJIEI Corporation  CD: 一柳裕之  Hiroyuki Ichiyanagi  D: 本間香衣  Kae Homma

Sfera スフェラ / インテリアショップ Interior Shop
SB: リコルディ アンド スフェラ Ricordi & Sfera  SB, DF: テン デザイン ラボ ten design lab  AD, D: 宮野琢也 Takuya Miyano / マーカス・モストローム Markus Moström

LUSH  ラッシュ / 化粧品の製造・販売  Cosmetic Manufacturer
SB: ラッシュジャパン  LUSH JAPAN Co.,Ltd.  D: 小林香代子  Kayoko Kobayashi / 二口万弥  Maya Futakuchi

MARKS&WEB　マークスアンドウェブ / 化粧品・生活雑貨店　Cosmetics and Lifestyle  Supplier

SB: 株式会社マークスアンドウェブ　MARKS&WEB CO.,LTD.　CD: 松山剛己　Tsuyoshi Matsuyama

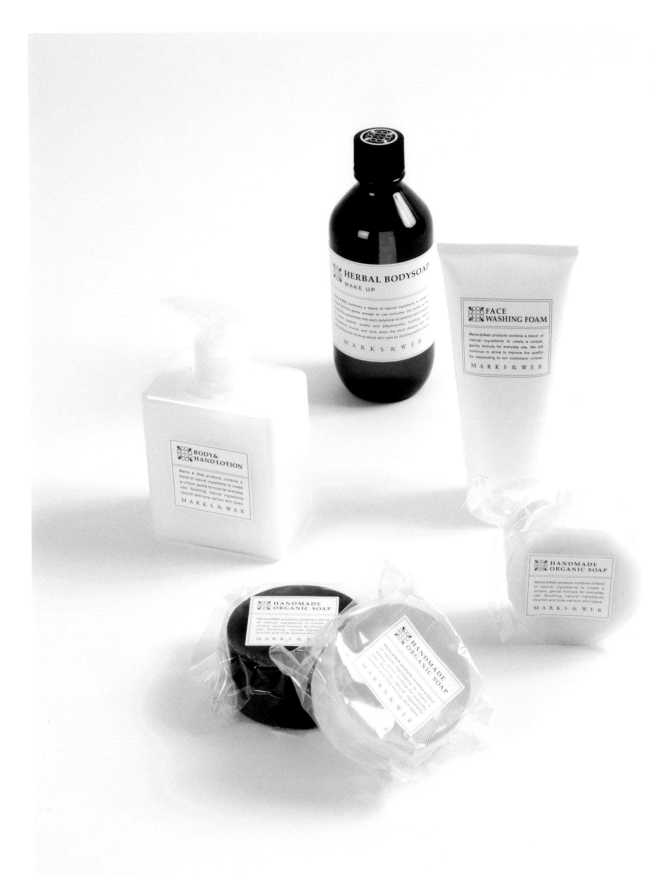

K-two ケーツー / 美容室 Hairdresser

SB, DF: 有限会社 DRIVE DRIVE,Inc.
CD, AD, D: 石井ゆみ Yumi Ishii

ir イール / 美容室 Hairdresser

SB, DF: 有限会社 DRIVE DRIVE,Inc.
AD, D: 芦谷正人 Masato Ashitani D: 石井ゆみ Yumi Ishii

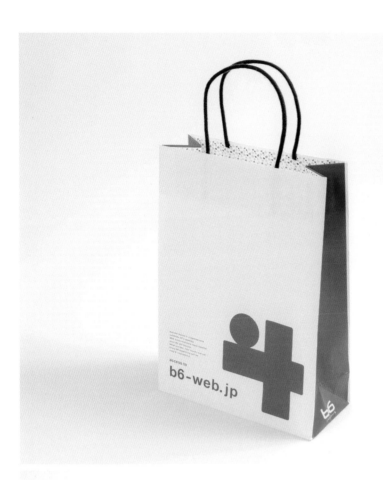

b6　ビーロク / ファッションビル　shopping complex

SB, DF: 有限会社 松下計デザイン室　Kei Matsushita Design Room
AD: 松下 計　Kei Matsushita　D: 田辺智子　Tomoko Tanabe

# SAINT JORDI FLOWERS THE DECORATOR サンジョルディフラワーズ ザ・デコレーター / フラワーショップ Flower Shop

SB: 株式会社ポジティブドリームパーソンズ Positive Dream Persons Inc.   CD, AD: 杉元崇将 Takamasa Sugimoto   D: 藤原祐介 Yusuke Fujiwara
DF: 株式会社ヘルメス HERMES INC.

conoka  コノカ / フラワーショップ  Flower Shop
SB, D, DF: デザイン オフィス アンダ  design office anda   Agent: 株式会社シー・レップ  C.REP co.,ltd.

環 TAMAKI / 漢方専門薬局 Chinese Medicine Drugstore

SB, DF: 有限会社 美澤修デザイン室 osamu misawa design room Co.,Ltd
CD, AD: 美澤 修 Osamu Misawa D, I: 梶谷聡美 Satomi Kajitani

3COINS スリーコインズ / 雑貨店 General Goods Store
SB, DF: 有限会社 松下計デザイン室 Kei Matsushita Design Room
AD: 松下 計 Kei Matsushita　D: 田辺智子 Tomoko Tanabe

# FOOD

**morozoff grand** モロゾフ グラン / 洋菓子の製造・販売 Confectionery Manufacturer

SB: モロゾフ株式会社 Morozoff Limited　CD, D: 服部滋樹 (グラフ) Shigeki Hattori (graf)
D: 松井 貴 (グラフ) Takashi Matsui (graf) / 大園貴生 (グラフ) Takao Ozono (graf) / 横山道雄 (グラフ) Michio Yokoyama (graf)

P (Shop): 下村康典  Yasunori Shimomura  Coordinator: 香西直美 (グラフ)  Naomi Kozai (graf)
Food Direction: 相原幸雄 (スタジオ カルティベイト)  Yukio Aihara (STUDIO CULTIVATE) / 藤本紀久子 (スタジオ カルティベイト)  Kikuko Fujimoto (STUDIO CULTIVATE)

continues >>>

117

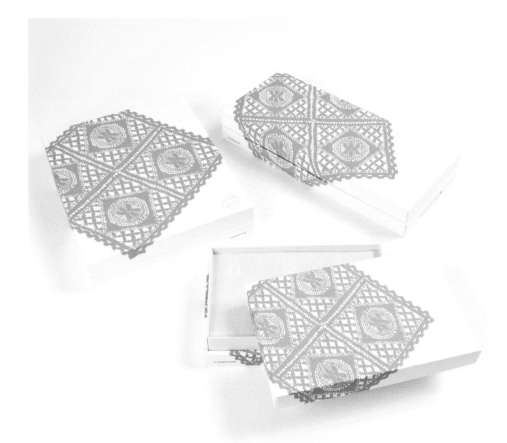

continues >>>

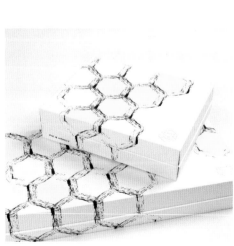

坂角総本舗 BANKAKU / 海老せんべいの製造・販売 Shrimp Cracker Manufacturer
SB: 株式会社 坂角総本舗 BANKAKU Co.,Ltd.

122

continues >>>

村上　MURAKAMI / 和菓子の製造・販売　Japanese Confectionery Manufacturer

SB: 合資会社 村上製菓所　wagashi-murakami Corporation

A

C

B

鼓月 **KOGETSU** / 和菓子の製造・販売 Japanese Confectionery Manufacturer

SB: 株式会社 鼓月 KOGETSU Co.,Ltd. CD: 山下知孝 Tomotaka Yamashita CD（A,C-E）: 家城浩幸 Hiroyuki Ieki AD（A,C-D）: 宮田忠彦 Tadahiko Miyata AD（E）: 高橋経一 Keiichi Takahashi
D（A,C-E）: 中村美穂 Miho Nakamura D（B）: 稲田美穂 Miho Inada DF（A,C-E）: 株式会社 第一紙行 DAIICHISHIKO CO.,LTD. DF（B）: 株式会社 鈴木松風堂 SUZUKI SHOFUDO CO.,LTD.

D

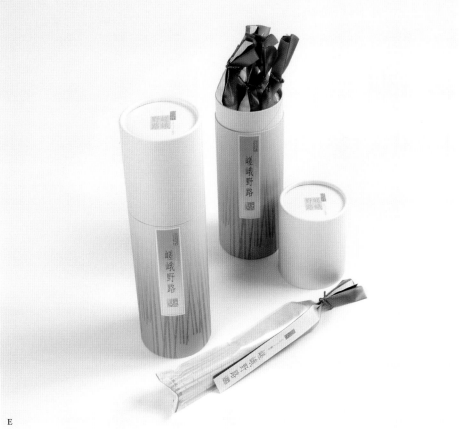

E

# MOCHI CREAM モチクリーム / 菓子の製造・販売 Confectionery Manufacturer

SB: 株式会社 ニッチ・インターナショナル Niche International Co.,Ltd.
CD, CW: 西村美玲 Mire Nishimura　AD, D: 湯栗紀子 Noriko Yuguri

BARBARA SWEETABLE バルバラ・スイータブル / カフェ / スイーツ  Cafe/ Patisserie

SB: 株式会社ポトマック  POTOMAK co.,inc.  D: 徳村有香  Yuka Tokumura

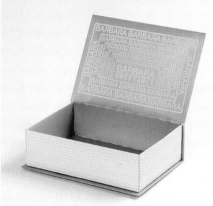

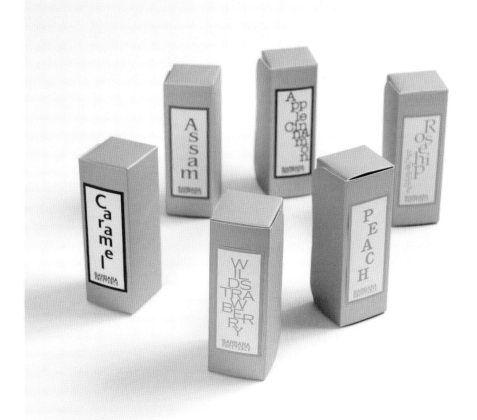

# PATISSERIE TOOTHTOOTH パティスリー トゥーストゥース / 洋菓子の製造・販売 Patisserie

SB: 株式会社ポトマック POTOMAK co.,inc.　D: 佐藤志保 Shiho Sato

あめや えいたろう　**Ameya Eitaro** / 和菓子の製造・販売　Japanese Confectionery Manufacturer

SB, DF: イエローデータ　YELLOW DATA　CD, AD, D: 岡部 泉　Izumi Okabe

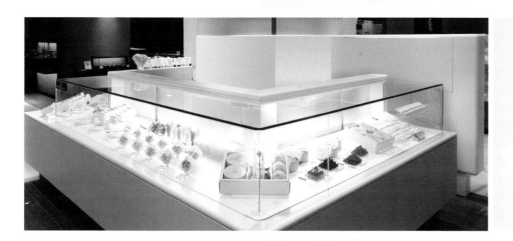

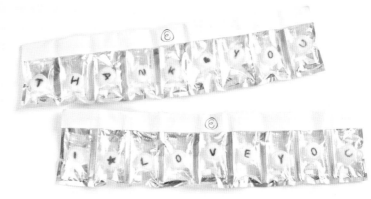

continues >>>

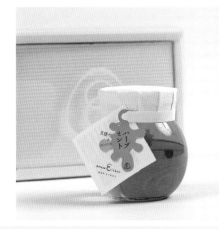

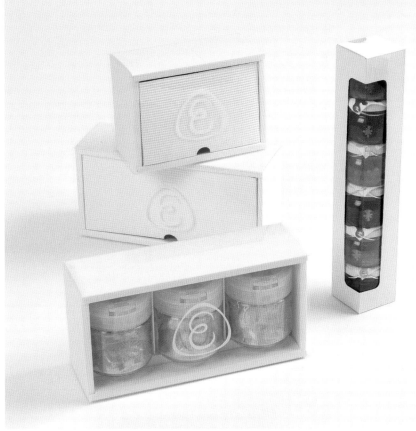

榮太樓總本鋪　**Eitaro Sohonpo** / 和菓子の製造・販売 Japanese Confectionery Manufacturer

SB, DF: イエローデータ　YELLOW DATA　CD, AD, D: 岡部 泉　Izumi Okabe

Factory Shin　ファクトリーシン / 洋菓子の製造・販売 Patisserie

SB: 株式会社シンケールス　SINCERUS Co.,Ltd.　CD: 小谷廣代　Hiroyo Kotani　AD,D: 園下健三（有限会社アスピリン）Kenzo Sonoshita (aspilin inc.)　D: 鈴木弘美　Hiromi Suzuki
P: 植田三代治（有限会社 植田写真事務所）Miyoji Ueda (Ueda Photo Office)　DF: 有限会社アスピリン　aspilin inc.

# DEAN & DELUCA ディーン＆デルーカ / フードセレクトショップ Fine Food Store

SB: 株式会社ディーンアンドデルーカジャパン　DEAN & DELUCA JAPAN

continues >>>

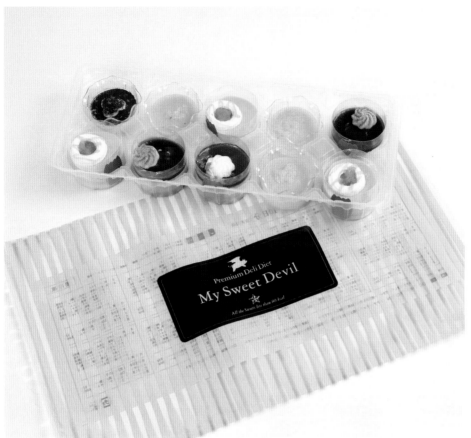

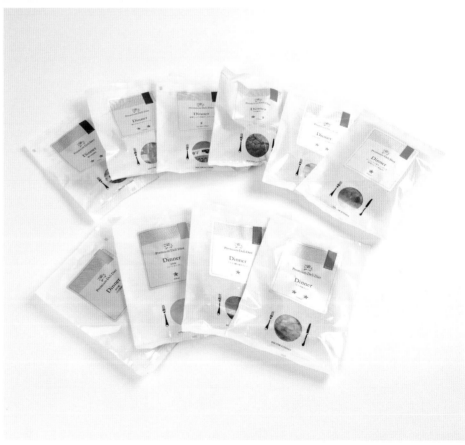

# Premium Deli Diet プレミアム デリ ダイエット / ダイエット食品の通信販売 Diet Foods Mail-Order

SB, DF: 株式会社 セルディビジョン  CELL DIVISION Co.,Ltd.

**beOrganic** ビーオーガニック / 総菜の販売 Delicatessen Sales
SB: 株式会社ロック・フィールド ROCK FIELD CO.,LTD.

# Chowder's  チャウダーズ / スープ専門店  Soup Shop

SB: 株式会社チャウダーズ  Chowders Corporation   DF: 株式会社エクスプレス  XPRESS Corporation

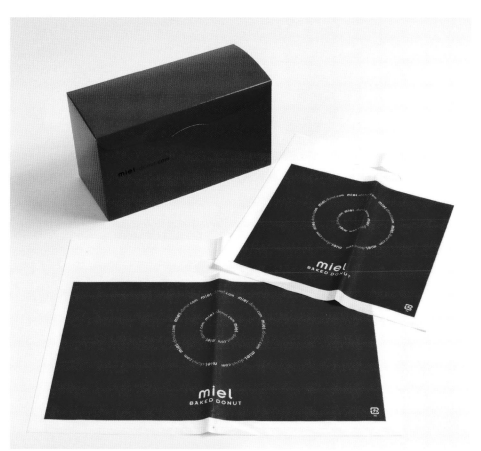

miel ミエル / 焼きドーナッツ専門店 Baked Donuts Shop
SB: ミエル miel

## DOUGHNUT PLANT ドーナッツプラント / ドーナッツ店 Donuts Shop

SB：株式会社ビッグイーツ　Bigeats & co.

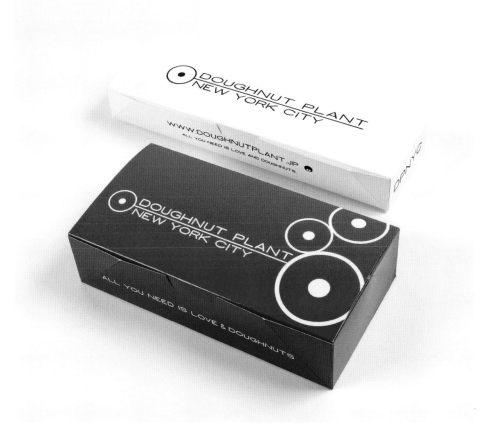

東京カレーラボ TOKYO CURRY LAB. / カレーをテーマにしたレストラン Curry Restaurant

SB, DF: グッドデザインカンパニー good design company　CD: 小山薫堂 Kundo Koyama　AD: 水野 学（グッドデザインカンパニー）Manabu Mizuno (good design company)
D: 上村 昌（グッドデザインカンパニー）Masaru Uemura (good design company) / 久能真理（グッドデザインカンパニー）Mari Kuno (good design company)

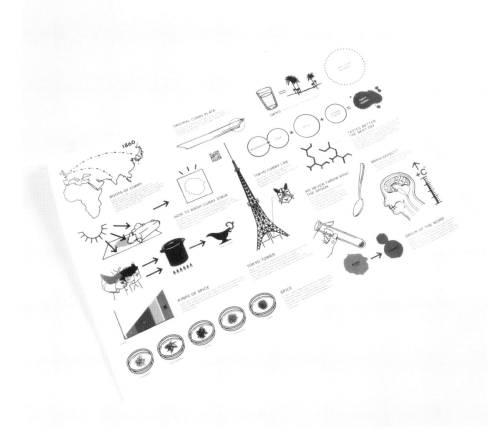

Panya des prés パンヤ・デ・プレ / ベーカリー Bakery

SB, DF: 株式会社コンプレイトデザイン COMPLETO DESIGN INC.   AD, D: 西村 武  Takeshi Nishimura

156

mango tree deli　マンゴツリーデリ / タイ料理のテイクアウト店　Thai Food Deli

SB: 株式会社 コカレストランジャパン　COCA RESTAULANT JAPAN CO.,LTD.

157

SHUMAI TARO

燒賣太樓 / 焼売専門店 Dumpling Shop
SB, D, DF: デザイン オフィス アンダ design office anda
Client: 株式会社 餃子計画 GYOZAKEIKAKU Co.,LTD.

ミートショップ ヒロ

**meatshop HIRO** / 精肉店 Butcher's Shop
SB, DF: 有限会社ティーピーオー TPO COMPANY
AD, Calligrapher: 田井祥文 Yoshifumi Tai D: 伊藤祐春 Sukeharu Ito

祇園鳴海屋

**Gion Narumiya** / 和菓子店 Japanese Confectionery Manufacturer
SB, DF: 有限会社ティーピーオー TPO COMPANY
AD, Calligrapher: 田井祥文 Yoshifumi Tai D: 伊藤祐春 Sukeharu Ito

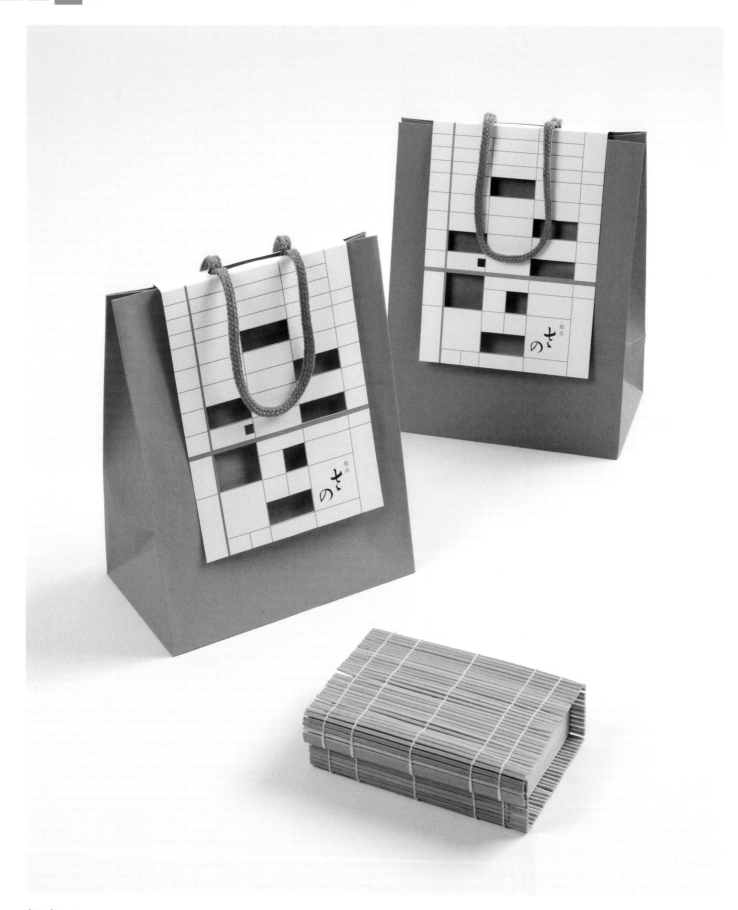

銀座 さの　Ginza Sano / 和食店　Japanese Restaulant
SB, DF: オジデザインワークス株式会社　ozi design works inc.

160

# INDEX

作品提供者一覧

164

NOW ON SALE

Shop Identity Series Vol.1

# SHOP CARD

ショップ アイデンティティ シリーズ Vol.1：ショップカードのデザイン

ISBN978-4-86100-501-5　定価（本体¥3,800＋税）

Shop Identity Series Vol.2

# SMALL PAMPHLET

ショップ アイデンティティ シリーズ　Vol.2：小型パンフレットのデザイン

ISBN978-4-86100-502-2　定価（本体¥3,800＋税）

Shop Identity Series Vol.3

Direct Mail

ショップ アイデンティティ シリーズ　Vol.3：DM（ダイレクトメール）のデザイン

ISBN978-4-86100-525-1　定価（本体¥3,800＋税）

ショップ アイデンティティ シリーズ Vol.4

# パッケージ&ショッピングバッグのデザイン

2008年3月23日　初版第1刷発行

[デザイン] 甲谷 一　　（Happy and Happy）
　　　　　　秦泉寺 眞妃（Happy and Happy）

[撮影] 谷本 夏（studio track 72）

[翻訳] 鎌田裕子（R.I.C. Publications）

[編集] 三富 仁 / 山下紫陽

[編集協力] 入江かおり


[発行人] 籔内康一

[発行所]
株式会社ビー・エヌ・エヌ新社
〒104-0042 東京都中央区入船3-7-2 35山京ビル1F
fax: 03-5543-3108　e-mail: info@bnn.co.jp
www.bnn.co.jp

[印刷] 株式会社 廣済堂

©2008 BNN, Inc.

ISBN978-4-86100-554-1
Printed in Japan